The United States

Illinois

Paul Joseph
ABDO & Daughters

visit us at
www.abdopub.com

Published by Abdo & Daughters, 4940 Viking Drive, Suite 622, Edina, Minnesota 55435.
Copyright © 1998 by Abdo Consulting Group, Inc., Pentagon Tower, P.O. Box 36036,
Minneapolis, Minnesota 55435 USA. International copyrights reserved in all countries.
No part of this book may be reproduced in any form without written permission from the
publisher.

Printed in the United States.

Cover and Interior Photo credits: Archive Photos, Peter Arnold, Inc., SuperStock

Edited by Lori Kinstad Pupeza
Contributing editor Brooke Henderson
Special thanks to our Checkerboard Kids—Annie O'Leary, Brandon Isakson, Raymond
Sherman

All statistics taken from the 1990 census; The Rand McNally Discovery Atlas of The
United States. Other sources: Compton's Encyclopedia, 1997; *Illinois*, Heinrichs,
Children's Press, Chicago, 1989.

Library of Congress Cataloging-in-Publication Data

Joseph, Paul, 1970-
    Illinois / Paul Joseph.
    p. cm. -- (The United States)
    Includes Index.
    ISBN 1-56239-858-X
    1. Illinois--Juvenile literature. I. Title. II. Series: United States (Series)
    F541.3.J67 1998
    977.3--dc21   97-12738
                                                     CIP
                                                     AC

Contents

Welcome to Illinois

Illinois is known as the Prairie State because of its flat grassland and treeless plains. The Prairie State, however, has become one of the most important states in the nation.

Illinois is a world **hub** for business and travel. The state is in the middle of the United States. It is south and west of Lake Michigan. The middle and southern area of Illinois has enough oil and coal to meet the needs of the entire world for more than 100 years.

In the northern half of Illinois are **industrial** cities like Rockford. Chicago, also in the north, is the third largest city in the United States, and is home to the tallest building in the world.

Most of the Prairie State, though, is farmland. The farm land in Illinois is some of the richest in the world. Illinois ranks third in the United States in exporting **crops**.

Some people call this wonderful state the Land of Lincoln. Illinois is where Abraham Lincoln became a lawyer, married, and was a **congressman**. Lincoln became the 16th president of the United States in 1860.

Tourists enjoy visiting Illinois because of the national parks, the wonderful land, the beautiful city of Chicago, and its people.

People come from all over the country to enjoy Illinois' beauty.

Fast Facts

ILLINOIS
Capital
Springfield (105,227 people)
Area
55,646 square miles
(144,122 sq km)
Population
11,466,682 people
Rank: 6th
Statehood
Dec. 3, 1818
(21st state admitted)
Principal rivers
Illinois River,
Mississippi River,
Ohio River
Highest point
Charles Mound;
1,235 feet (376 m)
Largest city
Chicago (2,783,726 people)
Motto
State sovereignty-national union
Song
"Illinois"
Famous People
Jane Addams, Walt Disney,
Ulysses S. Grant, Jesse Jackson,
Abraham Lincoln

State Flag

Illinois
Native Violet

Cardinal

White Oak

About Illinois
The Land of Lincoln State

Detail area

Wisconsin • Lake Michigan • Iowa • Illinois • Indiana • Missouri • Kentucky

IL

Illinois' abbreviation

Borders: west (Iowa, Missouri), north (Wisconsin), east (Indiana, Lake Michigan), south (Kentucky)

Nature's Treasures

The state's greatest treasure is its soil. With the help of a lot of rain during the growing season, the land **produces** large **crops**.

Illinois has around 83,000 farms. The most valuable crop grown is corn. The second is soybeans. Other important crops are, wheat, alfalfa, and different kinds of corn.

The state of Illinois produces a lot of beef. Sheep, chickens, eggs, and turkey are also raised there. The northern part of the state is known for its milk and other dairy products. Apples and other fruits and vegetables are grown in the south.

Other natural treasures in Illinois include **minerals**, especially coal and **petroleum**. Forests cover 10 percent of the state. The trees that grow there are oak, beech, hickory, and maple.

A farm in central Illinois.

Beginnings

The earliest people known to live in Illinois were the Mound Builders. They were **Native Americans** who left behind thousands of earth mounds they had built up from the prairie land.

When **Europeans** entered Illinois during the late 1600s they found many Native Americans living there. Some were the Cahokia, Kaskaskia, Michigamea, Peoria, and Tamaroa. By the 1830s most of the Native Americans were driven off their land and forced west of the Mississippi River.

The first **explorers** to cross the Illinois prairies were French explorers Father Jacques Marquette and Louis Jolliet. In 1673, they were at the site of Chicago.

A French settlement was founded in 1699. This became the first non-Native American settlement in

Illinois. In 1720, Illinois was owned by the French. In 1763, the land was turned over to the English.

In 1783, the United States took over ownership of Illinois. On December 3, 1818, Illinois became the 21st state. Vandalia was named the capital in 1820. In 1837, the capital was moved to Springfield where it still is today.

Father Jacques Marquette and Louis Jolliet.

Before 1500

The Land and People

The area of Illinois was a barren land with long stretches of treeless plains. The first known people to live in this state were the Mound Builders. These were prehistoric **Native Americans** who built mounds on this prairie land.

Many other Native Americans lived in Illinois. Some of them include the Cahokia, Kaskaskia, Michigamea, Peoria, and Tamaroa.

Illinois

Before 1500

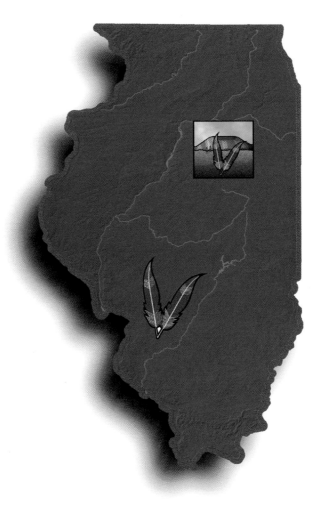

1600 to 1818

New Arrivals to Statehood

1600s: **Europeans** enter Illinois.

1720: The French take over Illinois.

1763: The area is given to the English from the French after the French Indian War.

1783: After Virginia claims Illinois in 1778, they give it to the United States.

1818: Illinois becomes 21st state on December 3. Vandalia is the capital.

Illinois
1600 to 1818

1860 to Now

President Lincoln to Today

1860: Abraham Lincoln, of Illinois, is elected as the 16th president of the United States.

1871: The Great Chicago Fire burns the heart of the city.

1937: Oil strikes in Marion County result in many people moving to Illinois.

1974: The Sears Tower, the world's tallest building at 1,454 feet (443 m), is completed in Chicago.

1997: The Chicago Bulls win their fifth NBA championship in seven years.

1860 to Now

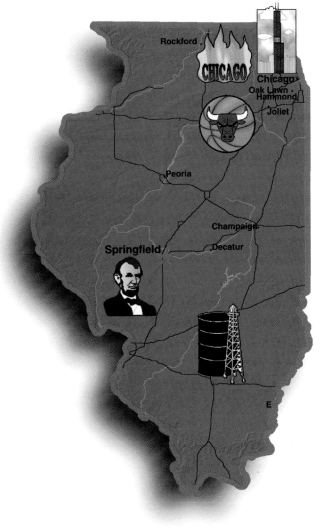

Rockford

CHICAGO

Chicago
Oak Lawn
Hammond
Joliet

Peoria

Champaign
Decatur

Springfield

E

Illinois' People

Abraham Lincoln is the most famous person from Illinois. Lincoln, the 16th president of the United States, was born on February 12, 1809. Lincoln was a lawyer and **Congressman** in Illinois.

In 1860, he was elected president of the United States. He **abolished** slavery and brought the country back together after the **Civil War**. Tragically, in 1865, he was **assassinated**.

The military commander of the Union in the Civil War was General Ulysses S. Grant. He lived in Galena, Illinois. Grant became the 18th president of the United States.

Today's most popular figure in Illinois is all-star basketball player Michael Jordan. The Chicago Bulls legend calls Illinois home during the season.

Other people who made Illinois home include 40th president of the United States Ronald Reagan, African-American activist Jesse Jackson, and Harold Washington, the first African-American mayor of Chicago. Bonnie Blair was the first American woman to win five gold medals in the Winter Olympics, and Patricia Roberts Harris was the first African-American woman to hold a **cabinet** position.

Jesse Jackson

Ulysses S. Grant

Abraham Lincoln

Splendid Cities

The wonderful city of Chicago is the third largest in the United States. Almost half the people of Illinois live in Cook County, which includes the city of Chicago. Because Chicago is in the middle of the United States, it is a great railroad, airline, and trucking **hub**.

Chicago sits on the tip of Lake Michigan. It has wonderful beaches, beautiful parks, and world-famous museums. It is home to the tallest building in the world, the Sears Tower. When you get to the top of the Sears Tower, you can see four states!

Rockford, the second largest city, is the main trade center of northwestern Illinois. Its products include tools, hardware, and furniture. Peoria, in the north-central part of the state, is a farming area on the Illinois River.

Springfield is the capital of Illinois. It is in the south-central part of the state. It is an important railroad center and farming region.

The city of Chicago with the Sears Tower in the background.

Illinois' Land

Illinois' size is 55,646 square miles (144,122 sq km) including 700 miles (1126 km) of water surface. The Prairie State is one of the flattest states in the country. Illinois is divided into three different regions.

The first region, the Central Lowland, is a region of sloping hills with broad, shallow river valleys. This area covers nearly all of the state. Charles Mound, the highest point in the state is in this region.

The second region, the Shawnee Hills, also called the Illinois Ozarks, enters the state from Missouri. It is located in the southwest corner of the state. This region forms a narrow set of hills along the Mississippi River.

The Gulf Coastal Plain, the third region, is a small strip of land on the very bottom of the state. This region, in Alexander County, has the lowest point in the state— 279 feet (85 m).

Illinois has a lot of grazing land for cows.

Illinois at Play

Illinois is one of the most visited states in the country, thanks to the city of Chicago. The rest of the state, however, offers many sites to see too.

The Prairie State offers many lovely bluffs and wooded **ravines** where people can hike. There are lakes and rivers that offer boating, fishing, and swimming.

There are beautiful state parks and many historical sites in Illinois. Most of the historical sites are about Abraham Lincoln. New Salem, where Lincoln lived for six years, has been made into a state historic site.

Chicago is located on Lake Michigan. By the lake there are paths where you can walk, jog, bike, rollerblade, or just sit and watch the boats. Not far from the lake are huge skyscrapers and a beautiful park.

Chicago also has fun museums and great entertainment. Chicago is known as the best professional sports town. You can go to legendary Wrigley Field and see the Cubs play baseball. On the other side of town the White Sox play at Comiskey Park. The Bears pack Soldier Field and fans love to see the Blackhawks play hockey at the United Center. The World Champion Chicago Bulls play there too.

Wrigley Field, where the Chicago Cubs play.

Illinois at Work

The people of Illinois must work to make money. Many of the jobs deal with **tourism** and service. Service jobs are cooking and serving food, working in stores, hotels, or restaurants. Chicago is also known world wide for businesses that deal with money.

The people of Illinois, mainly in Chicago, also work in **manufacturing**. Sixteen percent of the people in Illinois work in manufacturing.

One of the biggest manufacturers in Illinois is John Deere. They make tractors and other farm machines.

Outside of Chicago many people work as farmers. Illinois ranks among the leaders in farming. The biggest money-maker comes from the sale of livestock. Farmers also grow corn and other **crops**.

Illinois may be best known for a great president and a large city by the lake. But the Prairie State is also a great place to visit, live, work, and play.

The railroad yards in Chicago, Illinois.

ILLINOIS

Fun Facts

•Before Illinois was a state, the capital was Kaskaskia. When Illinois became a state in 1818, the first capital was Vandalia. In 1837, Springfield became the final capital of Illinois.

•The highest point in Illinois is Charles Mound. It is 1,235 feet (376 meters). The lowest point is along the Mississippi River in Alexander County. It is only 279 feet (85 m).

•Illinois is the 24th largest state. Its land covers 55,646 square miles (144,122 sq km).

Opposite page: The Mississippi River where it runs through Illinois.

Glossary

Abolish: to get rid of.

Assassinated: the murder of a very important person.

Cabinet: a group of people who work for the president of the United States.

Civil War: a war between people within the same country.

Congressman: a person elected by the people to represent them and make laws.

Crops: what farmers grow on their farms to either eat or sell or do both.

European: people who originally come from countries in Europe such as England, Germany, Italy, etc.

Explorers: people who are some of the first to discover and look over land.

Hub: the center of action.

Industrial: big businesses such as factories or manufacturing.

Industry: many different types of businesses.

Manufacture: to make things.

Minerals: things found in the earth, such as rock, diamonds, coal, etc.

Native Americans: the first people who were born in and occupied North America.

Petroleum: a liquid found in the ground that can be made into fuel.

Produce: to make.

Ravine: a long, deep, narrow valley.

Tourism: an industry that serves people who are traveling for fun, and visiting places of interest.

Tourists: people who travel for fun.

Internet Sites

Yahoo! Chicago
http://chi.yahoo.com
Metro Guide to Chicagoland.

Enjoy Illinois!
http://www.enjoyillinois.com
From this Web site you can plan your next Illinois weekend getaway —
and it's never been easier. Finding places to stay, restaurants, attractions,
events, outdoor adventures and more are just a click away!

These sites are subject to change. Go to your favorite search engine and
type in Illinois for more sites.

PASS IT ON

Tell Others Something Special About Your State

To educate readers around the country, pass on interesting tips,
places to see, history, and little unknown facts about the state
you live in. We want to hear from you!

**To get posted on ABDO & Daughters website
E-mail us at "mystate@abdopub.com"**

Index